small worlds

A SAGUARO CACTUS

Jen Green

CRABTREE
Publishing Company

Crabtree Publishing Company

350 Fifth Avenue
Suite 3308
New York, NY 10118

360 York Road, R.R.4
Niagara-on-the-Lake
Ontario LOS 1J0

Co-ordinating editor: Ellen Rodger
Commissioning editor: Anne O'Daly
Editor: Clare Oliver
Designer: Joan Curtis
Picture researcher: Christine Lalla
Consultants: Staff of the Natural History Museum, London
and David T. Brown PhD

Illustrator: Peter Bull
Photographs: John Cancalosi/BBC Natural History Unit, front cover, p 1, 8t, 11, 20, 27; Jeff
Foott/BBC Natural History Unit pp 10t, 10t inset, 10b, 19, 21, 25t; Tom Vezo/BBC Natural History Unit
pp 7, 22m; BBC Natural History Unit p 14; Bob & Clara Calhorn/Bruce Coleman Limited p 17; John
Cancalosi/Bruce Coleman Limited p 16; Jules Cowan/Bruce Coleman Limited, front and back cover,
p 9; Bruce Coleman Limited p 13; Corbis Images pp 3, 5, 6t, 8m, 12, 15, 22t, 23, 24t, 24b, 28;
Daniel Heuclin/NHPA p 26; John Shaw/NHPA p 18; NHPA pp 30, 31; Harry Smith
Horticultural Collection p 29.

Created and produced by
Brown Partworks Ltd

First edition 1999
10 9 8 7 6 5 4 3 2 1

CATALOGING-IN-PUBLICATION DATA

Green, Jen, 1955-
    A saguaro cactus / Jen green. — 1st ed.
    p. cm. — (Small worlds)
    SUMMARY: Describes the various animals that live in and around the giant Saguaro cactus in the
Sonoran Desert.
    Includes index.
    ISBN 0-7787-0134-4 (rlb)
    ISBN 0-7787-0148-4 (pbk.)
    1. Saguaro—Juvenile literature. 2. Saguaro—Ecology—Sonoran Desert—Juvenile literature. 3. Desert
animals—Habitat—Sonoran Desert—Juvenile literature. 4. Desert ecology—Sonoran Desert—Juvenile
literature. [1. Saguaro. 2. Desert animals. 3. Desert ecology. 4. Ecology.] I. Title. II. Series: Small worlds.
    QK495.C11 G689 1999
    583'.56—dc21

LC 98-51706
CIP
AC

Printed in Singapore

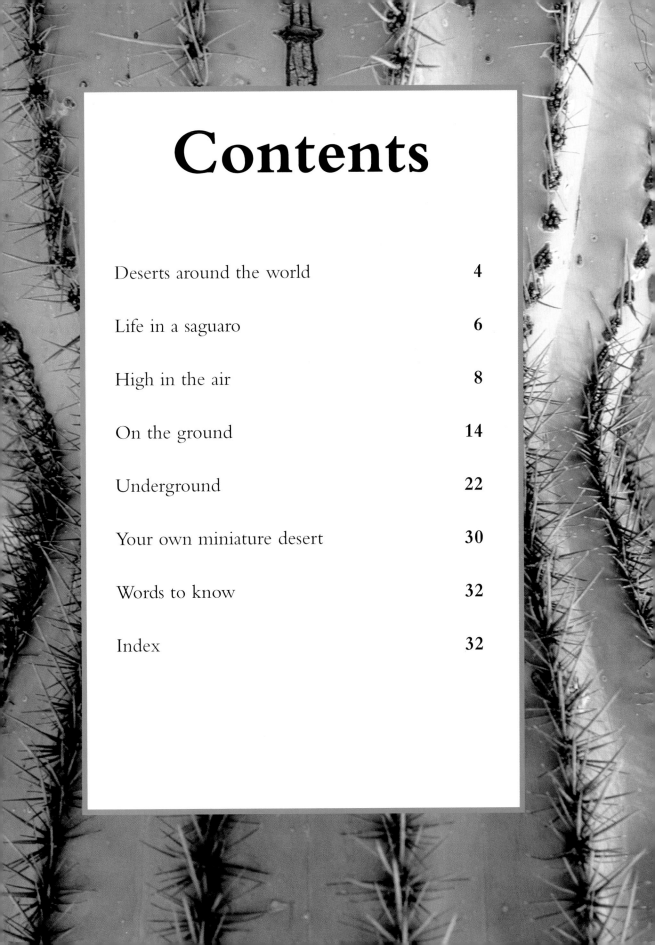

Contents

Deserts around the world

Deserts are dry places where very little rain falls. Some deserts receive no rain at all year after year.

▲ *Animals living in different deserts have adapted to the desert climate in similar ways. This fennec fox lives in the African Sahara desert. Like the North American kit fox, it has big ears that let body heat escape.*

Some deserts are very hot during the day, while others are very cold. In hot deserts there are no clouds to shield the land from the sun. The temperature can climb as high as 122°F (50°C). Because there are no clouds to trap the heat that builds up during the day, at night the desert gets very cold.

Deserts may seem like lifeless places, but many plants and animals live there. In this book you will meet some of the amazing creatures that live in and around a saguaro cactus. This giant plant lives in the deserts of southwestern North America.

▶ *Saguaro National Monument is a big nature reserve in southeastern Arizona. It covers 124 square miles (321 sq km). Forests of saguaros grow in this reserve.*

▶ *Most of the world's deserts lie on either side of the Equator, around the Tropics of Cancer and Capricorn.*

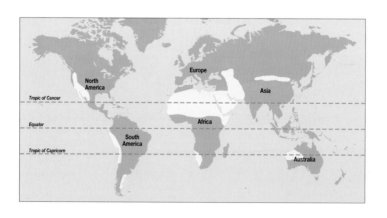

Life in a saguaro

The saguaro is a kind of cactus. Cacti are plants that live in deserts. Native to North and Central America, today cacti are grown all over the world.

The saguaro is the world's largest cactus. It can grow up to 56 feet (17 m) tall and weigh as much as an African elephant. This desert giant may live for 200 years, and its huge arms, or branches, only begin to sprout when it is about 70 years old!

The saguaro provides food, moisture, and shelter for all sorts of animals. Different parts of the plant provide a home for different types of animal.

On the ground
The base of the cactus shades and shelters ground-dwelling creatures such as the diamondback rattlesnake, the kangaroo rat, and the roadrunner.

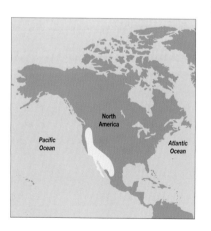

The Sonoran Desert in the southwestern United States and northern Mexico is famous for saguaros.

North America

Pacific Ocean

Atlantic Ocean

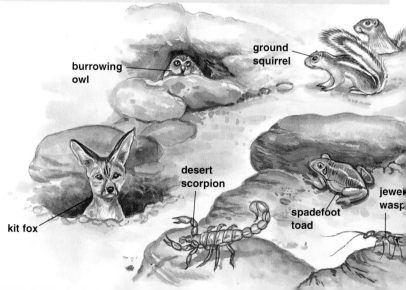

burrowing owl

ground squirrel

kit fox

desert scorpion

spadefoot toad

jewel wasp

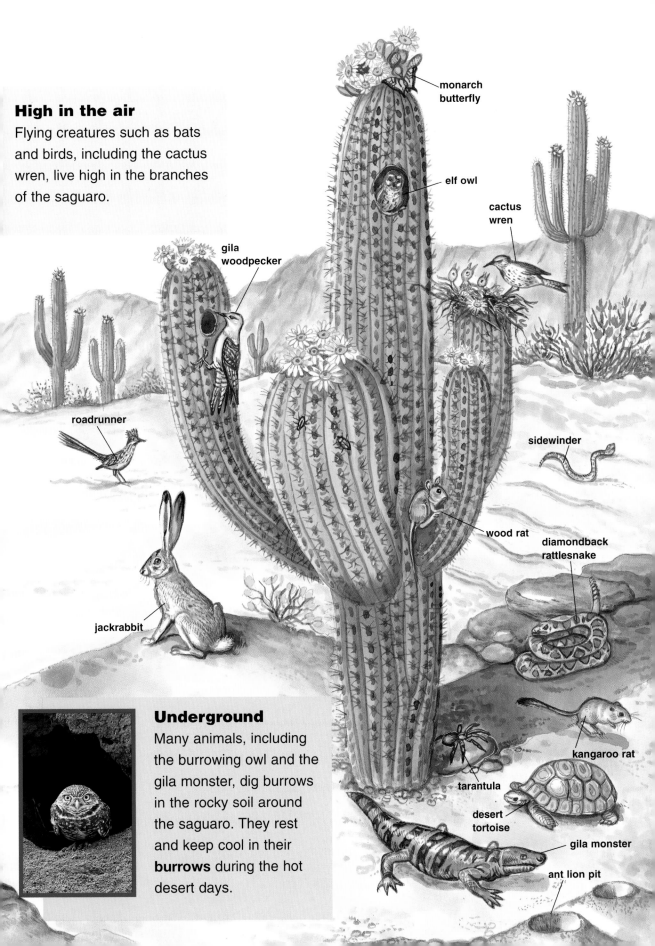

High in the air
Flying creatures such as bats and birds, including the cactus wren, live high in the branches of the saguaro.

monarch butterfly

elf owl

cactus wren

gila woodpecker

roadrunner

sidewinder

wood rat

diamondback rattlesnake

jackrabbit

Underground
Many animals, including the burrowing owl and the gila monster, dig burrows in the rocky soil around the saguaro. They rest and keep cool in their **burrows** during the hot desert days.

kangaroo rat

tarantula

desert tortoise

gila monster

ant lion pit

High in the air

Birds and bats flutter among the giant stems and spiny arms of the saguaro, hunting the small creatures that crawl there.

▲ The thorny spines of the cactus keep this Harris' hawk chick safe from predators when its parents go hunting for food.

▶ Cactus wrens make their home in the saguaro, too. Soft, cosy grasses keep the chill out on cold desert nights.

The cactus wren not only feeds on the bugs and lizards that scuttle around the cactus, it makes its nest there, too! This bird is specially adapted to its harsh **habitat**. Scaly legs protect it from the saguaro's spines. The wren does not need water to drink. It gets all the water it needs from the animals that it eats.

▶ No two saguaros are the same. As each one grows more branches, it creates its own unique shape.

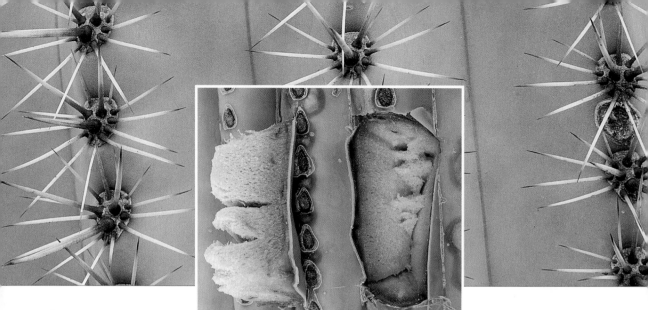

▲ The skin of the saguaro is tough and leathery, but inside, the flesh is juicy and full of sap.

▼ Saguaros do not begin to grow branches, like this one, until they are 70 years old.

Storing water

The saguaro survives in the desert by storing water inside its thick stems. The stems have pleats that expand like an **accordion** and fill up with water after rain. In dry periods they shrink back, as the plant uses up its stored water.

Plant food

Like all cacti, saguaros have no leaves. This stops the plant from losing too much water. Most plants use their green leaves and sunlight to make the nutrients, or food, they need to grow. This amazing process is called **photosynthesis**. Saguaros make their food without leaves. The plant uses its green stems for photosynthesis.

Sharp spiny tufts run down the ridges of the cactus, between the grooves. The spines protect the plant. They keep hungry animals from gnawing the stem for food and water.

Desert flower

In late spring, the saguaro blooms. The flowers open at night and wither the next day. The sugary **nectar** of the flowers attracts birds, butterflies, and long-nosed bats. As the visitors lick up the nectar, their heads are dusted with powdery **pollen** from the flower. When they move on to another flower, the pollen rubs off to **fertilize** the flower.

Night feeder

Long-nosed bats survive the searing desert heat by resting in the shade by day and being active at night. Animals that live like this are called **nocturnal**. Many other kinds of desert animals are night creatures.

▲ *This gila woodpecker is enjoying a delicious drink of saguaro nectar.*

▲ Male gila woodpeckers have a red patch on top of their head.

High flyers

Cactus wrens and Harris' hawks are not the only birds that can survive the harsh desert conditions.

Feathers are good protection against the sun's heat because they trap pockets of cool air next to the skin. Unlike most other animals, birds can fly long distances to find water, if they need to.

Using its strong beak, the gila woodpecker hollows out a nest hole in the stem of the saguaro cactus. The nest hole dries out to form a tough scab, which protects the saguaro's juicy flesh. The nest hole then becomes a dry, cool, safe place for the eggs and baby birds.

Like other woodpeckers, the gila has four toes. Two face forward and two face backward on each foot. Its stout claws keep a good grip on the cactus stem, while strong tail feathers help support the bird while it is climbing. The woodpecker eats beetles and other insects that crawl high on the saguaro's branches. Its favorite food is the grubs that burrow and live inside the stems. The woodpecker chisels out a little tunnel to reach the grubs, then licks them out with a slurp of its long tongue.

Borrowed home

The elf owl makes its home in a nest hole in the saguaro that has been abandoned by a gila woodpecker. Like most other owls, the elf owl is a nocturnal **predator** and only leaves its hole to hunt at night. Its large eyes help the bird to track down insects, spiders, and small lizards. Sometimes it hovers over a flower, flapping its wings to scare off any insects. As the frightened bugs take flight, the owl snaps them up in its beak!

FANTASTIC FACTS

● At just five inches (13 cm) long, the elf owl is the world's smallest owl.

● Like all owls, the elf owl coughs up neat pellets after feeding. The pellets contain bones and other indigestible bits.

◀ *During the day, the tiny elf owl stands guard at the entrance to its nest hole.*

13

On the ground

The base of the saguaro is home to many creatures that shelter from the heat in the shade of the giant plant. In the surrounding desert, smaller plants grow and flower after rain.

▲ *The desert scorpion is a deadly hunter. It poisons its victims with the stinger on the end of its tail.*

▶ *Like many other desert dwellers, the desert tarantula hunts at night. It hides under a stone by day.*

Unlike the saguaro, which lives for many years, many desert plants have only a short life. After a shower of rain, they sprout from seeds, come into flower and scatter their own seeds, all in a few days or weeks. Suddenly, the desert is a carpet of bright flowers. The plants then wither away and die, leaving their seeds in the ground, to shoot and grow after the next rain.

▶ *All plants need water. In the desert, the plants that live there all the time, such as saguaros, are widely spaced so that the roots of each one can gather enough water for the plant to grow.*

Survival tactics

The animals that live around the base of the saguaro must all cope with two main problems: the intense daytime heat and the lack of water. Most animals spend the hottest hours of the day hiding in the shade of plants and boulders. They find their food in darkness or at dawn or dusk, when it is cooler. Some animals that move around by day hop or run on tiptoe so that they do not burn their feet on the scorching earth.

Spiny nest

The wood rat is a vole that builds its big nest in a clump of cactus plants. The spiny prickles of the cactus protect the nest from enemies such as kit foxes. The nest entrance is so small, predators cannot reach in to catch the voles. During the hottest part

▼ *Wood rats are sometimes called trade rats. That is because they will pick up a shiny coin that is lying on the ground and leave in its place whatever they were carrying.*

of the day, wood rats sleep in cool, grass-lined chambers inside the nest. They come out at night to feed on seeds and on the fruit and flesh of cactus plants. Cactus flesh contains a poison that prevents most other plant-eating animals from feeding on it. Wood rats, however, have strong stomachs that are able to break down the poisons.

▼ *The kangaroo rat's tufted tail acts as a balance when the rat hops along.*

Desert hopper

The wood rat is a **mammal**, one of a large group of warm-blooded animals that nurse their young. The kangaroo rat is another small mammal that lives in the deserts of North America. It looks like the wood rat but has a long, bushy tail and very strong back legs that are shaped like the legs of a kangaroo. Kangaroo rats hop along on their powerful back legs just like miniature kangaroos! By hopping, the rats make sure that their bodies touch the hot desert soil as little as possible.

Outsize ears

Jackrabbits are hares that live in hot deserts and grasslands. Unlike many desert mammals, the jackrabbit does not dig a burrow where it can keep cool by day. To escape the heat, it rests in the shade of a boulder or tall cactus plant, with its ears pricked up. Heat escapes from the jackrabbit's body through its large ears. This helps stop the animal from getting too hot.

Jackrabbits feed on desert plants at

▼ *This black-tailed jackrabbit has ears that measure one-third of its total body length!*

dawn and dusk. Their long, sensitive ears pick up small sounds to warn of approaching enemies such as coyotes. At the first sign of danger, the hare takes flight. It can sprint along at speeds of 35 miles per hour (56 km/h).

Racing bird

The roadrunner is another champion sprinter. This bird is a better runner than flyer. It can race along the ground at 25 miles per hour (40 km/h). It was named for its habit of running alongside pioneer wagon trains, chasing the insects churned up by the horses' hooves. The roadrunner uses its speed to outrun its **prey**, which includes insects, mice, birds, lizards, and even snakes. Once caught, the prey are killed with a stab of the roadrunner's beak.

FANTASTIC FACTS

● Despite its name, the jackrabbit is a hare, not a rabbit. Unlike rabbits, which live in groups, hares tend to live alone.

● Roadrunners usually lay three to five eggs, but they have been known to lay as many as 12!

▼ *The roadrunner nests in the low branches of a small cactus or tree.*

Early warning system

The rattlesnake gets its name from the rattle at the tip of its tail. The snake shakes the rattle to warn its enemies of its deadly bite. The rattle is made of loose rings of hard skin. A new ring is added to the rattle each time the snake sheds its skin, so the oldest snakes often have the loudest rattles.

Fanged hunters

The rocks and stones around the saguaro cactus are home to several kinds of snakes. The eight foot (2.5 m) long diamondback rattlesnake is one of the most fearsome desert creatures. Its sharp fangs contain a poison powerful enough to kill a person.

The rattlesnake hunts at night, looking for small animals such as mice and rats. It picks up animal scents with the help of its forked tongue. Special tiny pits on either side of its head are sensitive to heat. The rattlesnake can sense heat given off by the bodies of its prey. It slithers closer to its prey, then strikes. Its fanged teeth inject a poison that quickly kills the prey. The snake then swallows its victim whole.

The sidewinder is a small desert snake that has a unique way of moving. It slithers sideways by throwing its body into a series of loops. At any time, only a small part of the snake's body touches the hot desert sand. You can tell when a sidewinder has passed by in the desert, because it leaves a trail of curved lines in the sand.

▲ *The poison shoots out through holes in the tip of the rattlesnake's fangs. It is stored in a sac inside the snake's head.*

▼ *The sidewinder is small compared to the diamondback rattlesnake. At most, it grows to 30 inches (75 cm) long.*

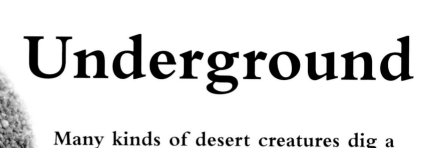

Underground

Many kinds of desert creatures dig a burrow and live underground. Below the surface, it is cooler, so animals seek shelter there from the sun's scorching heat.

▲ *The ant lion larva makes deep pits in the sand. As it digs, it piles the sand on its head then tosses its load clear of the hole.*

▶ *The burrowing owl can make a noise like a rattlesnake to frighten away an enemy entering its burrow!*

The burrowing owl usually finds a hole abandoned by another creature. But if it cannot find a likely spot, it digs its own burrow with its razor-sharp claws. Unlike most owls, it hunts by day and sleeps by night. Instead of flying, it sometimes runs along the ground to catch its prey.

▶ *At dawn, the desert sky is hazy and the temperature is cooler. In just a few hours, the land will become very hot.*

▲ The ground squirrel puffs out its tail and holds it over its body to make a sunshade.

Keeping out of the sun

Ground squirrels are furry rodents that live underground in large groups called colonies. They dig a whole network of tunnels that runs far beneath the desert soil. At the hottest parts of the year, the squirrels go into a deep sleep called **hibernation**.

Foxy hunter

The kit fox rests by day in its deep underground burrow. Like its cousin, the African fennec fox, it has large ears that lose heat to keep the animal cool. At night, the fox hunts insects, rabbits, mice, and lizards, using its good hearing and excellent sense of smell. It is also called the swift fox, because it can run so fast. Sadly, this fox is becoming rare in North American deserts.

Armored shell

The desert tortoise is another burrowing creature. It digs out its cool, dark lair with its flat front legs. The hard shell on its back is

The colors and patterns on the tortoise's shell blend in with the desert, making it hard for predators to spot.

made up of about 60 bony plates joined together. The shell shields the tortoise from the hot sun and protects it from enemies. When danger threatens, the tortoise simply draws its scaly head and legs inside.

The tortoise moves far too slowly to chase after prey. It feeds on juicy cactus, biting though the spiny flesh with its horny jaws.

These kit fox cubs will stay in their mother's burrow until they are around 15 weeks old.

A saguaro cactus

▶ *Gila monsters grow up to two feet (60 cm) long.*

Deadly bite

The gila monster is one of the few lizards in the world with a poisonous bite. The bright orange-and-black patterns on its scaly skin warn enemies that it is dangerous. The lizard's fat tail stores food in dry periods when food is scarce. The gila monster hunts small mammals, birds and their eggs, and other lizards. It tracks down prey by smelling them with its long, flickering tongue.

A shimmering jewel

The jewel wasp is a desert insect with a greeny-blue body that shines like a jewel. The female wasp works hard to feed her

FANTASTIC FACTS

● Adult jewel wasps feed on nectar, not meat.

● The bug "meat" that the jewel wasp lays her egg inside does not go bad. The wasp's sting contains an antiseptic that stops the flesh from rotting.

young. She digs a burrow and then goes hunting among the cacti. When she catches an insect such as a cockroach, she paralyzes it with her sting. She then drags her victim into the burrow and lays an egg on it. When the larva (young wasp) hatches, it feasts on the bug meat.

In cold blood

Lizards, tortoises, and snakes are **reptiles**. All reptiles are cold-blooded. This means their body temperature is about the same as their surroundings, unlike warm-blooded animals such as birds and mammals, which can keep an even body temperature.

Snakes and lizards, like the collared lizard, below, must bask in the sun in the early morning to warm up before they can move about and hunt. During the sweltering heat of the desert at midday, they move into the shade to stop their bodies from overheating.

▲ *The male spadefoot toad grows to about three inches (7.5 cm) long.*

Race against time

Frogs and toads are water-loving amphibians that live near ponds and streams. You would not expect to find them in the desert, yet spadefoot toads live there. For about ten months of the year, these toads sleep underground in deep burrows dug out with their spade-shaped feet. After a shower of rain, the toads emerge. They mate and lay eggs in rainwater pools. After only two days, tadpoles hatch out from the eggs and start to feed. The tadpoles grow up more quickly than the young of other toads, because they must become adults before the rainwater pools dry up. As the water vanishes, the young toads dig themselves into the damp sand and begin the long wait for the next shower of rain.

Lying in wait

The ant lion is a burrowing insect and a good desert hunter. The adult has a long, thin body and two pairs of wings. The larva has a fat, wingless body and a big head with fierce jaws. The larva traps other insects, such as ants, by digging a cone-shaped pit in the sand, often near a cactus. It lies buried in the sand at the bottom of the trap, waiting for its victim. When an unwary ant falls into the pit, the ant lion pounces and seizes the creature in its spiky jaws!

FANTASTIC FACTS

● Spadefoot tadpoles take just two weeks to become adult toads.

● Ant lion larvae are also called doodlebugs.

● Adult ant lions look like dragonflies.

◀ *Each funnel-shaped ant lion pit can be up to two inches (5 cm) deep and nearly three inches (7.5 cm) wide.*

Your own miniature desert

Even if you live nowhere near a desert, you can bring a little bit of the desert into your home. Why not become a desert detective, find out about desert rats that make good pets, or even grow your own cacti?

▼ *Gerbils are relatives of the wood rat. They live in sandy parts of Africa and Asia, but they also make popular and friendly household pets.*

Cacti are easy to grow from seed. Buy a packet of seeds at your local nursery. Prepare your seed pot by putting a layer of gravel at the bottom, then filling the pot with seed compost, mixed with a little sand. Sprinkle with water, then

scatter the seeds on top. Cover with a plastic bag, and put the pot in a warm, shady place. Once the seedlings appear, remove the bag. When your seedlings are bigger, transplant them into their own pots. Keep cacti in a warm, sunny place, and remember, these desert plants do not need much water.

BE A DESERT DETECTIVE

1 Now that you know about desert weather, you can compare it with the weather where you live. Keep a diary of daily weather conditions.

2 Buy or borrow a thermometer. Take readings of the temperature in the shade and in the sun each day. Make a chart to show your findings.

3 Place a beaker outside and use it for measuring rainfall. How many inches fall each day? In the desert, less than 10 inches (25.4 cm) fall in a year!

◀ *Cacti that you can grow at home come in all shapes and sizes. They are all the miniature relatives of the giant saguaro.*

Words to know

accordion A musical instrument with folding bellows.
burrow A tunnel in the ground where an animal lives.
fertilize When a male sex cell joins with a female sex cell.
habitat The place where a plant or animal lives.
hibernation A deep sleep.
larva An immature insect.
mammal A warm-blooded, hairy animal that raises its young on mother's milk.
nectar Sweet food made by plants to tempt insects.

nocturnal Describes an animal that sleeps or rests by day and is active at night.
pollen Yellow powder made by the male part of a flower.
photosynthesis Process by which plants make their own food, using the energy in sunlight.
predator An animal that hunts other animals for food.
prey An animal that is eaten by another animal.
reptile A cold-blooded, scaly, air-breathing animal.

Index